Introduction

This is Freda Land's second collection of illustrated poetry, following on from her first book 'Memories in the Attic'.

'Sentimental Journey' is a lovingly warm and sometimes funny, collection of poems which captivate life's everyday events. Events we can all relate to at one time or another.

Added to this collection are the fantasy dreams that have entertained the writers quieter moments.

We hope the journey you are about to make through the pages of this book will rekindle memories and raise the odd smile.

Bob Wilson
Editor

JOURNEY

First published in 1999 by

Wilbek & Lewbar
90 Victoria Road, Devizes
Wiltshire, SN10 1EU

Author   Freda Land
Editor   Bob Wilson
Illustrations   Ted Sibbick
Design & Layout   Emma Wilson

Printed in Great Britain

ISBN 1 901284 20 4

Dedication

This book is dedicated to the memory of my Mother and Father.
Also, with special thanks to my husband Malcolm for all
the encouragement given to me and, for putting up with
me scribbling away at midnight!

Not forgetting my sister Pauline - who, got me into this
'fine mess' in the first place. Thanks Pauline for talking
me into writing and giving me a new life!

Contents

The magic teddy bear

The children had a secret, which their parents did not know,
It was about their favourite teddy bear, whose name was Figaro.
One ear was mostly missing, he had also lost an eye,
So a button had been sewn on instead, just to help him to get by.

His fur had seen much better days, but did it really matter?
The children loved him as he was, though his clothes were now in tatters.
One day while the parents watched T.V., the children played in their room,
Then Figaro suddenly came to life, and his little voice did boom!

"My name is Figaro!" he said, "I am a magic teddy bear,
I can sing and dance for you, if your parents are not here.
I am a little deaf, because your cat has chewed my ear near off,
Perhaps you can make me a new one, from the fluffy coat in the loft!"

The children agreed, and stealthily got, the coat of imitation fur,
And a large ear was cut for Figaro, with a pair of blunt scissors.
Industriously the ear was sewn onto Figaro's head that day,
And all the while, the parents dozed, through a television play.

The children took the bear downstairs, to show their mum and dad,
So when their dad jumped in the air, they thought he had gone quite mad.
"That was mum's new coat," he said in shock, "I bought it yesterday,
It was a surprise for tomorrow, for her thirtieth birthday!"

But the deed was done, what could they do? but see the funny side,
And Figaro stayed quite silent, his one eye open wide!

By Freda Land

The grandfather clock

The grandfather clock, it told the time, but not just of today,
Inside its case was a little book, telling of all its yesterdays.
It was first made in eighteen ninety, that many years ago,
And over the years had kept good time, being rarely fast or slow.

The first owner was a German man, living in London town,
He was first attracted to the clock, when he heard its chiming sound.
He passed it on to his youngest son, whom auctioned it away,
A man from Cornwall bought it, having been in London for the day.

It had pride of place in his home, but then alas, he died,
And the house, it passed to a cousin, with contents left inside.
The cousin did not want the clock, again for sale it went,
This time purchased by a Welsh man, living somewhere near Gwent.

He kept the clock for twenty years, but then took it away,
To a shop that sold antiques and books, and there two years it stayed.
Eventually it was purchased by a young woman, around the age of twenty eight,
And now she is its guardian, as it awaits its fate.

By Freda Land

The rocking chair

In the corner sat the rocking chair, it was very old,
But ever time I went past it, I felt deathly cold.
Was it my imagination, or did I really see,
An old man sat there in it, and was he watching me?

He was aged near enough to eighty, his hair was short and grey,
He wore a dark brown three-piece suit, of the nineteen twenty days.
A fob watch was in his pocket, on a lovely golden chain,
And a walking stick was in his hand, a stout one of dark grain.

His legs were short, his shoes shone bright, and he always tapped a foot,
Perhaps he tried to catch my eye, but he knew I would not look.
One day whilst looking at old photographs, his shadow over me came,
It fell upon a railway scene, with a man waving from a train.

Realisation came! it was great uncle Joe, whom had once resided here,
But he had gone into an old folks home, when his end was very near.
He used to sit out on the porch, whilst rocking away he would read,
So his ghoust came home, to the place he loved never again to leave.

By Freda Land

The tramp

He wandered down the old back road, his coat shabby and damp,
But no one even glanced at him, for he was just a tramp.
At litter bins he stopped and searched, scraps of food to find,
Mouldy bread, or rotten fruit, he did not seem to mind.

His hair was long and matted, a beard was on his face,
Bloodshot eyes looking tired of life, in need of a better place.
In his pocket was a bottle, liquid held there in,
Likely to be methylated spirits, there was no cash for gin.

His eyes did search a garden and latch upon a shed,
Had he found a shelter for the night? he did not have a bed.
His boots were old and dirty, no laces were in sight,
And he carried a grubby blanket, that once had been pure white.

I felt so fit and healthy, as I did pass his way,
Not wishing to ignore him, so politely said "good day!"
A deep cultured voice then answered me, much to my surprise,
And a smile showed up a handsome face, lighting up those bloodshot eyes.

I wanted to ask him about his lot, but went upon my way,
Dropping a few coins on a dustbin lid, so for a meal he would be able to pay.
Then I walked into my comfortable home, which was neither cold nor damp,
And felt engulfed with pity, as I thought about the tramp.

I ran back out, but he was gone, the coins had gone as well,
Hopefully they would be spent on food, there was no way I could tell.
I doubt he will pass this way again, continuing to survive,
Depending on 'Mother Natures' mercy, to help him stay alive.

By Freda Land

The gift of life

Why are we here? a million times this question is asked and still we do not know,
We are not even sure from whence we came, or even where we go.
Yet most are formed so perfectly, generations passing down,
Bearing similarities to relations, perhaps a smile, or maybe a frown.

We accept our complex bodies, hearts pumping each second of the day,
Yet when we get a single pain, we want it to go away.
In vanity strive to look perfect, not too fat, yet not too thin,
Change hair colour, clothes and make-up, according to the mood we are in.

We accept the talents given, perhaps we can sing, or dance, or act,
And take our ability to reason, as all so matter of fact.
Architecture, engineering, to take our world forward every day,
But what is the final purpose? there is no one who can say!

Some countries fail, to value each person's gift of life,
And it is lost in war and conflict, in diplomatic strife.
Our gift of life is given with love, and love is what carries life on,
The love we have for each other, the next generation brings on.

Perhaps we will never know, not even in death, the reason why we live,
But while we are here, we can take part, and to others happiness give.
So every morning we can wake up, and maybe thankfully say,
Whatever the reason for life on this earth, we are grateful for the new day.

By Freda Land

A Working man

He walked slowly down the old pit path, he had worked a twelve hour day,
He always worked sixty hours a week, to earn his meagre pay.
He longed to quit his mining job, but his family had to be fed,
So he had his dinner, sat an hour, then went upstairs to bed.

He arose at five, to start at six, and work his arduous day,
Amid the darkness and the dust, that was eating his lungs away.
His mates all worked in silence, they too, did yearn to leave,
With dreams of working in the sun, their senses they deceived.

He had very few days holiday a year, and did not go away,
A coach trip to the seaside, was the excitement of the day.
A pint of beer on a Saturday night, along with friends he would sit,
Some gardening on the Sunday morning, and Monday back to pit.

He never did reach sixty, silicosis had set in,
And life without the working man, for the family was grim.
For life in the nineteen twenty's, was no better than today,
But he lay at peace when the strikes began, to fight for better pay!

By Freda Land

The ghost of a jester

In the castle was a jester, to amuse the Earls and Lords,
But even a court jester can sometimes be lost for words.
One day he ceased to amuse the guests, the Earl, he was displeased,
So made the jester crawl around, on his hands and knees.

Then came a shout from someone, but from whom he could not tell,
"Let us take this silly jester and throw him down the well!"
No sooner said, then it was done, the jester left to die,
For he had broken arms and back, and twisted legs and thigh.

He lay in pain for three whole days, until he gasped his last,
But swore to avenge his awful death, in an outpouring of wrath.
Three months passed when someone claimed, to have seen him one dark night,
Leaning over the old Earl's bed, who promptly died of fright!

With moans and cries he would be heard, when darkness did befall,
And fear of what he planned to do, struck terror into all.
Two Lords were talking late one night, out on the balcony,
They both were found the following day, their deaths a mystery.

Gradually all the people left, the castle became a shell,
And stories spread both near and far of the jester and the well.
A knight was known to venture there, when feeling brave and bold,
Sensing an evil air around the well, it made his blood run cold.

The castle still stands, and so too the well, in ruin and decay,
Yet the laughter and cries of the jester, can still be heard today.
And as the evening closes in, it is not a trick of light,
If you should see a ghostly figure, rise from the well each night.

By Freda Land

Snow

Snowflakes softly falling, falling from skies as black as night,
Covering all with gentle touches, forming a coat of white.
Dancing and swirling, the snowflakes get thicker, carpeting the ground,
Tiny specks landing all around us, without a single sound.

"Come and touch me!" say the snowflakes, "just hold out your hand,
I will change myself to water, then to moisten land.
I will cloak the bulbs beneath me, protect them from the cold,
I will form a world of beauty, for you to now behold!"

Now the snowflakes, thick and heavy, start to fall with speed,
Out come children, to make snowmen, to the cold they pay no heed.
Out come men, with heavy sledges, to sloping fields they go,
Out come dogs to run and tumble, revelling in the snow.

Thick and fast the snow has fallen, ten inches in one day,
Folk stay at home and enjoy the comfort, "can't get to work!" they say.
Snow so fresh, so pure and white, perfect and pristine,
Nature momentarily changing clothes, from its usual coat of green.

By Freda Land

Summer is late this year

Summer is late this year, the skies are full of rain,
The garden soggy with water and there are puddles down the lane.
The breeze is cool, of the sun there is no sign, the sky a deepening grey,
And the birds stay strangely silent, no summer here today.

The tiny plants are in the ground, and long to grow up strong,
But need the warmth of sunshine, to help them get along.
The fruit trees have all lost their flowers, and little fruits appear,
They need the sun's rays to bring them on, but summer is late this year.

Holidays are booked down by the sea, the children want to play,
But mum fetches them a colouring book, saying "you had best stay in today!"
Later on to a leisure centre they all go, the swimming pool gets the vote,
But not quite the same as being in the sea, in their little dinghy boat.

But wait! the sky is clearing, signs of blue are showing up high,
And clouds that were so low and grey, have now gone floating by.
At last! a watery sun appears, oh! how a scene can change!
And hasty plans drawn up for the day, can now be rearranged.

The sun grows stronger, just feel the warmth! the difference that it makes!,
Already the sound of voices, around the boating lake.
And splash, there's someone in the sea! children start to play,
Don't waste your time, come join the fun, summer has come today!

By Freda Land

The joy of birds

I love the birds in my garden, they are such a joy to see,
They sing their songs, and chirp away, bringing happiness to me.
The robin, with his blood-red breast, his little life not much over a year,
Yet he is such a lovely little bird, our lives to brightly cheer.

The blackbirds are so very tame, and trill out to be fed,
While the blue tit's like the peanuts, not interested in the bread.
Chaffinch and bullfinches appear, to see what there is to eat,
And sparrows hang around all day, perched on the garden seats.

Starlings, jackdaw's, all drop by, and woodpeckers fly in,
We always know when they are about, their cry makes such a din!
They tap the trees, then fly away, but not for very long,
All gathering again, near the end of the day, perhaps to hear the blackbird's song.

The jay makes a rare appearance, the wren is always near,
But all do carefully stay up high, with cats their greatest fear.
Squirrels also come for the peanuts, and their antics makes me laugh,
They turn the feeder upside down, to empty out the lower half.

With greenfinch, yellow hammer, siskin too, the garden abounds with life,
And watching them I pick out pairs, which ones are 'man and wife'?
I think the birds are a special gift, mother nature has given us,
But if you are still not sure, then rise at dawn, and hear the birds chorus.

By Freda Land

Ghost walk

While wandering down a leafy lane, in calm and solitude,
I met a stranger by a gate, who broke in upon my mood.
"Good afternoon", the stranger said, "It's such a lovely day!"
"Yes," I replied, "not a cloud in the sky", and then went on my way.

But the stranger caught up quickly, and we were walking side by side,
Passing two handsome horses, which children were preparing to ride.
We came upon a cottage, "old Rose lived here!" I said,
"She was sat under her apple tree, when someone found her dead."

The stranger smiled, "I knew her well," her voice almost a whisper,
I glanced a curious look at her, could this be Rose's sister?
"Rose had a secret no one knew!" the stranger then did say,
"And no one's ever known of it, at least until today.

Although she lived a simple life, she had a lot of wealth,
But thought nothing of goods and money, she was content and in good health.
There is a box buried deep in the garden, beneath the apple tree,
With deeds and bonds, also a will, and lots of jewellery."

"Really," I said, "well, that's a surprise, no one around here had known,"
But there was no reply from the stranger, I was walking all alone.
No sign of her up or down the lane, she had vanished in thin air,
Then I realised it was Rose's ghost, who had been talking to me there.

By Freda Land

Secret place

I wonder if you have a secret place, hidden within your mind,
Where you retreat to rest yourself, when the world gets too unkind.
Is it a peaceful garden, with a rippling stream beyond,
Or a seat under a willow tree, watching ducks on the village pond?

Are you high up on a mountain, seeing scenes which give delight,
Or do you take a stroll along a beach, in the brightness of moonlight.
Are you rowing on a peaceful lake, in silence except for birds,
Or do you call out in a valley, where your echo can be heard.

Perhaps you are in a Cathedral, and feel a peace within,
Not just a place where people go, to confess their earthly sins.
To see the stained glass windows, their beauty shining out,
And the stone carvings of the gargoyles, made so thick and stout.

Where ever you go, in your secret place, that only you will know,
I hope it brings a restfulness, and allows your worries to go.
So take a few moments for yourself, retreat into your mind,
Maybe then the dark shadows will lift, making the world seem more benign.

By Freda Land

A storm at sea

The crew they screamed for mercy, but the sea said "none today! "
And placed another gigantic wave in the battered galleons way.
The galleon fought back bravely, but the storm was much too strong,
And all the valiant sailors knew that the ship did not have long.

The rocks grew ever closer, the main mast moaned and creaked,
Sails all torn and flapping, and the storm still had not peaked.
The captain tried with all his might, his ship to safety steer,
But the wind wailed like a banshee, the devil sensing victory near.

Then with a mighty cracking sound, the mast hurtled to the deck,
Underneath it lay the look-out, with twisted, broken neck.
The galleon then gave a sickening lurch, and a rock did find its mark,
Sinking swiftly was the galleon, into waters cold and dark.

The crew climbed into tiny boats, to row desperately away,
But only ten were left alive, by the cruel seas that day.
They reached the safety of the cliffs, and clung to higher ground,
With tortured eyes they watched the ship go down, and fellow sailors drown.

Then gradually the sea it calmed, a victory it had claimed,
And for losing the galleon, cargo and crew, the captain would be blamed.
But he would never know that, for he lay deep below,
In Davy Jones's locker, where many sailors go.

By Freda Land

Forever him

In every hour of every day, he comes into your head,
And your mind turns over all the things, that he has ever said.
You want to know his every thought, his views on all of life,
To understand him from a boy, his struggles and his strife.

To walk with him, and talk with him, to shop and sit to eat,
And still ask a thousand questions, whenever you both meet.
To smooth his hair, gaze in his eyes, to touch his hands and face,
To listen to his laughter, feel the warmth of his embrace.

You would choose to spend your life with him, if ever he should ask,
And you know from deep within your heart, your feelings they will last.
Of all the people you have met, how is it he is the one for you?
But from the first time that you met him, you knew that this was true.
'It's love'.

By Freda Land

Make believe

Sometimes to children their toys are real, in their world of make believe,
Making up stories beyond belief, with no intention to deceive.
Dolly is ill and is put to bed, there she has to stay,
Where she waits until the doctor comes, while her owner goes out to play.

Teddy, like daddy, has to go off to war, his helmet placed upon his head,
A stick for a gun, because daddy said, 'without one he would be dead'!
Teddy waved goodbye to the other toys, as they wiped away their tears,
For teddy and daddy, there is a good chance they may not be back for years.

Toy dog Ben has a new lead, and is taken for a walk,
Twice a day he is taken out, but if only he could talk!
Industriously now, Anna washes and irons, the motions so real to see,
It's amazing how quickly each little child learns, for Anna is only aged three.

Now there's an island surrounded by sea, so you must be careful where you step,
Around the corners of the room you walk, so as not to get your feet wet!
The imagination of a young child, is a wonder to behold,
What a shame that we each grow to be adults, and don't play when we are old!

By Freda Land

Jasper Zebedee

Jasper Zebedee was his name, and cider was his brew,
With five pints of that inside him, there was now't he couldn't do.
Old Rosy really fancied him, and wanted him to wed,
But Jasper wanted a single life, and not a double bed!

One night there was a party, to celebrate the hay was in,
The villagers knocked the cider back, and created such a din,
Old Jasper, well, he'd had his fill, so on a haystack he did lay,
When Rosy jumped up beside him and had her wicked way!

The outcome was, as months went by, Rosy began to swell,
But would Jasper marry her? that was something none could tell.
For he and his dog, Scrumpy, had an easy kind of life,
With no plans in mind for Jasper, to ever take a wife.

Old Jasper, he got in a sweat, whatever could he do?
He had no love for Rosy, his heart knew this was true.
But he still had his dignity and thought of family pride,
So went off to see Rosy, to make her his new bride.

He stood there quaking in his shoes, as she opened up her door,
"Why Jasper!" she looked so amazed, "What be you coming for?"
"Well Rosy, you're with child and I know it's mine", he said!
"So I think that it's only proper, that you and I should wed".

"Oh Jasper! it 'ain't yorn", she said, "from the haystack that one night,
I only went and touched your belt, and you fainted out of fright.
I took off all your clothes, to cool you down and give your body air,
But Billy Wright came after me, and we got on real fair!"

Jasper went off, oh so relieved!, the happiest of men,
And drank down his first cider, and then another ten!
But he made himself a brand new rule, which he's kept right to this day,
Not to rest on top of the haystack, while he's out there baling hay!

By Freda Land

Homemade wine

Have you ever tasted it, some lovely homemade wine?
Well, if you haven't, come round here, and have a taste of mine!
Mind you, don't knock it back like lemonade, for this is powerful stuff,
And when you get out in the air, you will know you have had enough!

There's elderberry, plum and blackberry, rose petal, redcurrant too,
And the lovely sparkling elder flower, just right for me and you!
Someone I know drank quite a lot and was leaning on a door,
But then her legs went in the air, and she was laid out on the floor!

There's orange, apple, gooseberry, pear, I find sloe a little dry!
Carrot and hop make a good one, and peach brandy is worth a try!
Try rhubarb or some raisin wine, raspberry is a lovely brew,
Or dandelion or parsnip, whatever might suit you!

My brother in law came for a tasting, but wine is a deadly thing,
He was seeing two of everything next morning , and it was making his head sing!
Crab apple is a lovely sweet one, or there is strawberry, and mangold is quite fair,
And the mixed up fruits, called 'summer wine', a bottle not to share!

So buy your demi-john, sugar and yeast, sterilisation tablets too,
And you will soon be on the road, to making homemade brew!
Whatever your choice, enjoy a glass, you will soon be feeling fine,
And no doubt see the pleasures, in making homemade wine!

By Freda Land

The artist

Walking near a meadow, on a warm and sunny day,
I came across an artist painting, beside the small pathway.
He was looking at the old brown barn, which was near to falling down,
His study of it was so intent, and his forehead showed a frown.

I tiptoed by, but curiosity won, so I said "may I see?"
He smiled and said "yes, take a look!" and turned the easel to face me.
I had a shock, just stood and stared, for where the barn had been,
He had seen something other than I had, a beautiful coaching Inn!

It was timber beamed, an ancient place, with character and style,
While just in front, four horse's paused, to eat and rest awhile.
Alighting from the coach, he had sketched a woman's faint outline,
But he had lost the theme of finishing the detail of her design.

"She is old!" I said, "with brown brogue boots, and wears a large gold brooch,
And by her side is a tiny child, clutching at her long thick coat.
In his other hand he holds a toy, it looks like a teddy bear,
The child is dressed in a little suit, and has lovely, short blond hair!"

"That is it!" he cried, and started to sketch, and then looked up to say,
"My name is 'Matthew John Sinclair', and I am on holiday!
I came to paint a meadow scene, but the barn seemed to cast a spell,
Though why I have sketched the coaching Inn, I cannot hope to tell!"

"There was a coaching Inn here once," I said, "they razed it to the ground,
For sheltering a highwayman, whom they later found.
They took him out and hanged him, on the oak tree over there,
And it is very odd that his name too, was Matthew John Sinclair!"

By Freda Land

The wizard

In the land of wizardry, was one who reigned supreme,
He knew each person's every thought, and also every dream.
The brave would stand before him, those who had travelled far,
To see the magic workings of the wizard named Lanpar.

His mystic secrets known to none, he lived his life alone,
But kept a mighty dragon, which he allowed to roam.
The blackest night he would light up, flashing rainbow colours through the sky,
While sounds like thunder filled the air, his wizardry he would try.

He was at war with Fremal, a demon whom he despised,
And planned for hours to find a way, on Fremal to bring demise.
Then late one night he left his tower, and flew on dragon's wing,
Over the top of Fremal's fort, and began to chant and sing.

Fiery arrows left the skies, shooting downwards like torrents of rain,
And Fremal's warriors ran out, their armour all aflame.
Fremal himself was then to show, his talons reaching far,
But flying high above his head, in safety rode Lanpar.

Then Lanpar came down to the earth, and faced the evil demon,
To kill this vile and deadly thing, all his wizardry he would summon.
The fight was long and gory, Lanpar grew tired and weak,
Fremal had brought in other beasts, with sharp and cruel beaks.

So the wizard called upon his magic spear, that answered only right,
It pierced the demons wicked heart, and he died that dreadful night.
Their leader gone, the rest did run, and the tale it spread afar,
Of how the demon king was killed, by the wizard named Lanpar.

By Freda Land

Is anybody out there

There is somebody out there, I am sure it must be true,
If it was proven there was no one, how dull for me and you.
Not to think of frightening fiends, or creatures far in space,
Nothing at all even similar, to our perfect human race.

Would they want to eat us? we have no protective shell,
If they started on the overweight, they would do very well!
So many U.F.O. sightings, and people whisked away,
To have odd experiments done to them, and returned in the same day.

I can see my favourite creature, large head, and huge green eyes,
Not much of a nose, and a tiny mouth (too small for 'people' pies)
A thin neck, long arms, four fingers, twice the length of ours,
He is from an unknown planet, much further on than Mars.

His body is short and rounded, he wears no clothes at all,
But is able to speak every language, and also plays football!
So please, if someone is out there, it would be very nice to see,
You drop by for a bite to eat, as long as it is not me!

By Freda Land

The spider

He lives there in the greenhouse and for a special treat,
Knowing I am afraid of him, he will run across my feet.
Then climb onto the work bench, and sit in my seed tray,
He knows that I will not touch him, and will have to go away.

Then later on, if I would venture back, the seeds to try to plant,
He will see me coming, and again make his advance.
He is very large and hairy, with little beady eyes,
His body fat and rounded, so my fear is no surprise.

He has lived there several years now, and although sometimes wanders out,
Makes a point of going back inside, if he knows I am about.
I have named him 'Horrid Harry', and will stare right at his face,
But when he moves toward me, I always run out of the place!

I know he has his purpose, but I still have my fears,
And have lived with 'Horrid Harry' for far too many years,
So I will have to take the greenhouse down, and have a lawn instead,
And hope that 'Horrid Harry' never turns up in my bed!

By Freda Land

Burnt offerings

Dear Joannie! how she loved to cook, but every meal was a woe,
A few mouthfuls would get tasted, then into the bin it would go!
She tried to bake an apple pie, but the crust was black and charred,
And even her rice pudding, had edges crisp and hard.

Her potato chips were soft and white, her custard always lumpy,
No wonder that her husband Ted, always seemed so grumpy!
Her ocean pie was all ocean, no fish was to be seen,
And her cabbage ended up near white, instead of a healthy green.

Her souffle flat, roast beef cindered, but still she forged ahead,
And many a time her husband, ill, had taken to his bed.
Her gravy cut out with a knife, looking grey upon the plate,
A turkey waiting to be stuffed, thanked God it had already met its fate!

Her sponges lay like slices of bread, never did they rise,
And you never knew what you would find, inside one of her mince pies!
For if she ran out of a filling, she would try 'some other thing',
It's been known she used honey and bread crumbs, and then her wedding ring fell in!

Things came to a head, when poor Ted died, and Joannie's curry got the blame,
The coroner said he'd never seen internal organs looking so inflamed!
So Joannie was sent off to prison, where life got very grim,
For someone said she was a cook, and so was selected for catering!

By Freda Land

How do you measure

How do you measure a loving heart, or eyes that show they care,
How do you measure the gentle touch, of fingers in your hair.
How do you measure the softest voice, that calms your fears and woes,
How do you measure feelings, that from deep within you grow.

How do you measure caring thoughts, or encouragement to strive,
How do you measure faith and hope, that helps you to survive.
How do you measure laughter, or the sound of a voice that sings,
How do you measure beauty, like the pleasure a flower brings.

How do you measure the gift to hear, the sound of a young child's voice,
How do you measure a brain that reasons, for you to make a choice.
How do you measure movement, that lets you walk and play,
How do you measure breathing, every second of each day.

How do you measure sunshine, or even rain and hail,
How do you measure snowstorms, or breezy winds and gales.
How do you measure the deep blue sea, or clouds up in the sky,
How do you measure fields of green, and trees that grow up high.

How do you measure soft brown earth, which gives us food to live,
How do you measure up our God, who has so much to give.
All these things are given to us, all things from him on high,
If the one above ever takes us back, how will he measure you and I?

By Freda Land

A winter's walk

The frost lay thick as a snowfall, the air was crisp and cold,
Garden shrubs coated in glistening ice, a picture to behold.
Birds with fluffed out feathers, hopping round, some food to find,
Gladly eating up bits of bread, and scraps of bacon rind.

The walk to the lane was silent, no cars did come that way,
Hedgerows filled with lacy cobwebs, on which the frost did stay.
A watery sun appeared above, but no warmth from it I felt,
And neither did the shrubs or trees, for the frost it did not melt.

The earth covered by a carpet of white, my feet making a crunching sound,
Startling a few brave rabbits, as they sat on the wintry ground.
The birds above were singing, their songs were loud and clear,
A lovely start to the morning, at the coldest time of year.

By Freda Land

The crowning of a queen

I had only ever seen the one, so could scarce believe it true,
A leafy glade was filled with fairies, gnomes, sprites and pixies too.
Rolled out on the grass, a carpet of gold, with threads of shiny green,
And at the end of the carpet, a single gold chair, to seat the fairy queen.

Four gnomes were dressed as ushers, in suits of velvet cream,
And welcomed guests as they arrived, for the crowning of the queen.
There was lots of noise and chatter, excitement rising high,
Then she arrived, the queen to be! on her favourite dragonfly.

Her dress was made of silver web, a star was in her hair,
She smiled and waved to everyone, as she walked to the golden chair.
The time had come, with no show of pomp, on her head was placed the crown,
So she took off her star, shook it over her guests, sprinkling stardust all around.

The sight was oh! so beautiful, shimmering stardust flying high,
Raining down on each and all, not one did it pass by.
The queen thanked the guests for coming, inviting them to the evening ball,
I stayed and watched in amazement, determined to see it all.

Their wine was made from rose dew, collected at first light,
And the meal was stamens of flowers, which they ate with great delight.
Musicians played, the sprites did dance, and fireflies flew around,
The pixies, elves and fairies swirled, their feet not touching the ground.

The evening air filled with laughter, the moon shone full and bright,
I had never seen such happiness, as in the glade that night.
If all the folk on earth could see, if only in a dream,
The fairies, gnomes and pixies, when they crown a fairy queen.

By Freda Land

Perhaps... One day!

I long to visit far off lands, that abound in mystery,
Perhaps I will travel through the air, or take a trip by sea.
I would like to see the pyramids, or gaze at Hadrian's wall,
And take a year to wander round, making sure I see it all.

The snow capped Alps and mountain roads, plants that please the eye,
With people helping me understand, however they get by,
Living with famine, through years of drought, scavenging what they can,
Perhaps spending some time with aid workers, who help out fellow man.

To see the North Pole, and huge polar bears, in their natural environment,
Or the safari parks of Africa, maybe camping out in a tent.
To go up in space, looking down on earth! how exciting that would be,
Try a trip by balloon, or go down deep below, seeing life within the sea.

To travel the wide world over, the people I'd get to know,
From Europeans and Aborigines, to the less known Eskimo.
Absorbing new cultures, new surrounds, enjoying the new sensations,
Using my mind to understand our planet, and all of its wonderful creations.

Perhaps... One Day!

By Freda Land

Sentimental Journey

I used to live here years ago, when I was just a child,
Remember running through the fields, past the broken stile.
My cousin once got chased by the cows, when her leg was set in plaster,
I can see her trying to hurry on, hear our raucous laughter.

The fossils that we found in coal, containing ferns, and creatures, too,
Taken home, then lost again, so off to find some new.
Making dams in the little stream, and paddling up and down,
Picking hazelnuts in the woods, when the shells had all turned to brown.

Flying kites, without much success, picking blackberries to eat,
Having fun playing "kick the tin", up and down the street.
Repeating all our tables, in the village school,
Learning to swim the breaststroke, in the local swimming pool.

The happy childhood days have passed, to adults we all grow,
But it s nice to recall the memories, of all those years ago.
The children now have a different world, modern things to do and see,
Computer games are now "their thing", with videos, and TV.

By Freda Land

The old tobacco pipe

He loved to puff on his old pipe, whilst telling of a tale,
The aroma of the tobacco lingered, making his clothes smell stale.
But he would bring out fables, of bold, courageous knights,
And tell of days of Camelot and warriors sent to fight.

The Knights of the round table, stories of Lancelot,
Merlin and Arthur, also brought into the telling of the plot.
We sat in awe and wonder, spellbound by the old man's voice,
And would choose to live in Camelot, if we ever had the choice.

All of us were under ten, and sat upon the ground,
And he would stop and glare at us, if we ever made a sound.
For twenty minutes, every night, we would go the old man's way,
To hear a fresh new story, then we went on our way.

As time went by he'd take deeper breaths, to draw on that old pipe,
Contentment written on his face, as he told his tale each night.
Sometimes we would take an apple, as a way of thanking him,
And a toothless face would show a smile, partly hidden by a whiskery chin.

Over the years he told us, legends, fables and tales,
Of fishing boats and pirates too, of porpoises and whales.
Of ogres, wizards and demons, and sometimes we would take fright,
And covered our heads with bedclothes, so we would not dream at night.

When he passed on, we lost a friend, but he left us a legacy,
A love of stories to broaden our minds, and a knowledge of history.
His house was left to the nation, and was full of relics of old,
But the memories he left to us children, became more precious than gold.

By Freda Land

Illustrated Poetry Books

Other Poetry Titles in the series:

Dreams of the Raven	ISBN 1 901284 01 8	£3.00 inc p&p
The Spirit of Christmas	ISBN 1 901284 08 5	£3.50 inc p&p
Circles of Love	ISBN 1 901284 03 4	£3.50 inc p&p
Memories of a Wiltshire Farmer	ISBN 1 901284 04 2	£3.50 inc p&p
Memories of a Wilts Farmer Wife	ISBN 1 901284 15 8	£3.85 inc p&p
Meditating Dreams	ISBN 1 901284 07 7	£3.75 inc p&p
This Wonderful World	ISBN 1 901284 06 9	£3.75 inc p&p
Life's a Laugh	ISBN 1 901284 09 3	£3.75 inc p&p
Life's Little Miracles	ISBN 1 901284 10 7	£3.75 inc p&p
Earth's Rhapsody	ISBN 1 901284 11 5	£3.85 inc p&p
Candlelight Visions	ISBN 1 901284 14 X	£3.95 inc p&p
Memories from the Attic	ISBN 1 901284 13 1	£3.95 inc p&p
Spirit of a Loving Heart	ISBN 1 901284 16 6	£3.95 inc p&p
Whispers in the Garden of Dreams	ISBN 1 901284 17 4	£3.95 inc p&p
Wings of the Brave (RAF)	ISBN 1 901284 12 3	£4.00 inc p&p
Bombers' Moon (RAF)	ISBN 1 901284 18 2	£4.25 inc p&p
Straight from the Heart	ISBN 1 901284 19 0	£3.95 inc p&p

If you would like to know more about our illustrated poetry books or order any of the above titles (cheques payable to Wilbek & Lewbar), then do contact us at:

Wilbek & Lewbar
90 Victoria Road, Devizes, Wiltshire, SN10 1EU, England
Tel / Fax: 01380 720271   E-mail: wil.bar@zetnet.co.uk